THE GREAT RACE MAZE

ANNA NILSEN

For Auntie Anne
- From ATB

Published by Little Hare Books
45 Cooper Street, Surry Hills
NSW 2010 AUSTRALIA

First published in 2002

National Library of Australia
Cataloguing-in-Publication entry

Nilsen, Anna.
  The great race maze.

  For children.
  ISBN 1 877003 07 7.

  1. Maze puzzles – Juvenile literature. I. Title.

793.73

Designed by Louise McGeachie and Kerry Klinner
Printed in Hong Kong
Produced by Phoenix Offset

5 4 3 2 1

GET READY TO RACE AROUND THE WORLD!

The race begins at the green flag 🚩 on the left-hand page, which marks the starting point. Navigate your way through the mind-bending maze as fast as you can to reach the red flag 🚩 on the right. Then turn the page and find the next green flag to start the second exciting lap of the race…

ON YOUR MARKS

Beware – danger, detours and hazards await you! (Don't worry if you get lost along the way – the solutions are at the back of the book.) If you survive to the end, then test your skill with the 12 extra puzzles that follow the last maze.

GET SET

Time yourself over each section of the race, and see how long it takes you to complete the whole hair-raising journey. Keep a note of your times and try to improve on your record. You can play against a friend and see who wins. Good luck!

NOW GO!

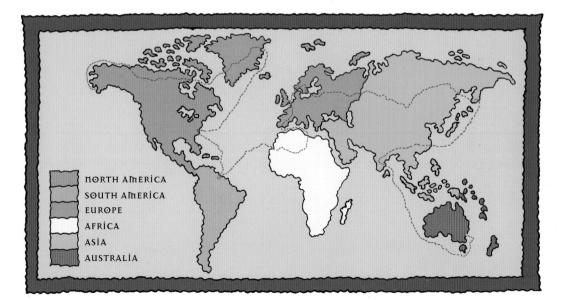

NORTH AMERICA
SOUTH AMERICA
EUROPE
AFRICA
ASIA
AUSTRALIA

THE ARCTIC

Sail through icy seas, race along pipes and logs – you might even have to travel by dogsled to reach the waiting jet.

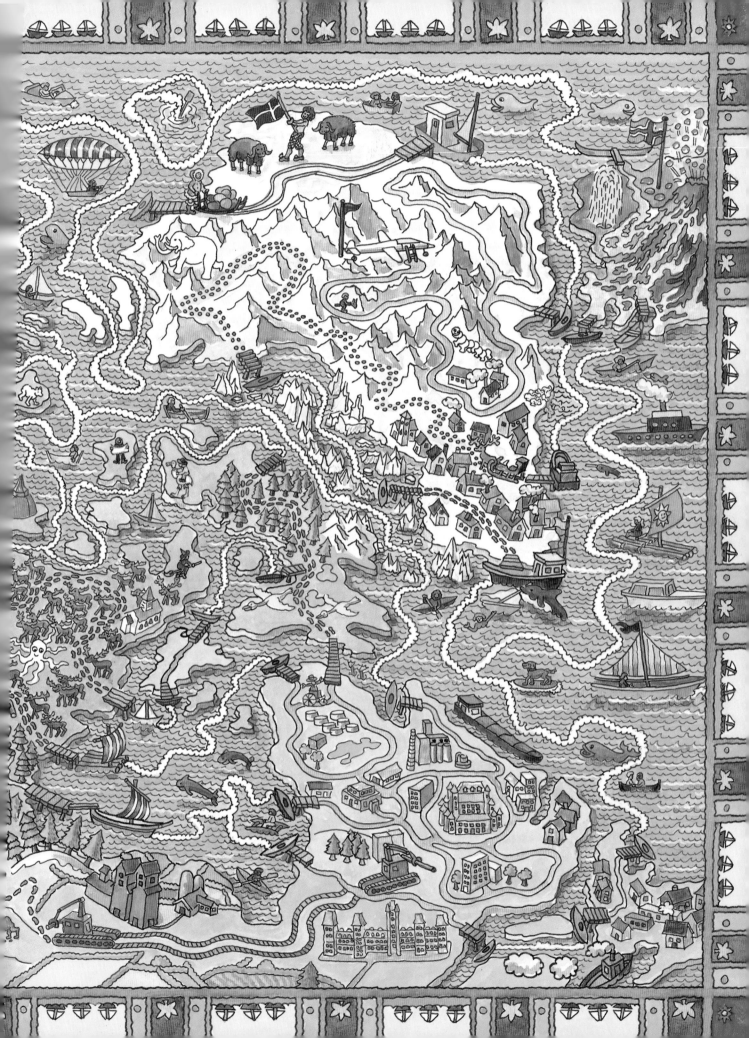

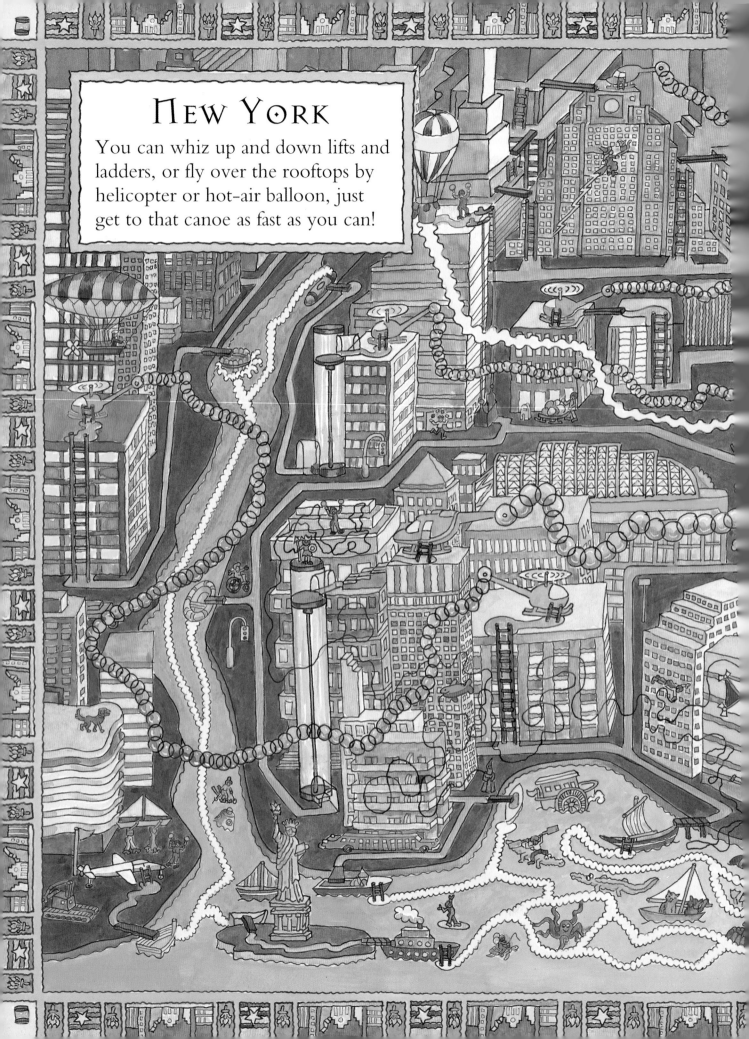

NEW YORK

You can whiz up and down lifts and ladders, or fly over the rooftops by helicopter or hot-air balloon, just get to that canoe as fast as you can!

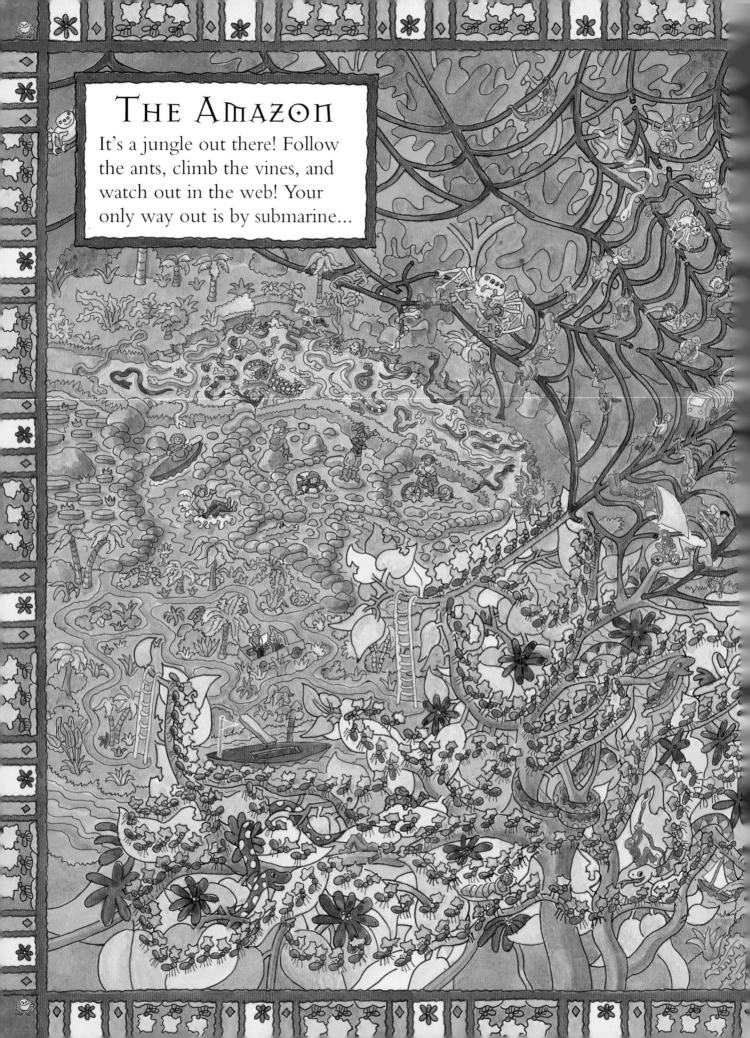

THE AMAZON

It's a jungle out there! Follow the ants, climb the vines, and watch out in the web! Your only way out is by submarine...

THE ATLANTIC

You're really in deep water now! But if you can follow the tangled rope to the surface, there's a raft waiting to give you a lift.

North Africa

Travel by sea, track footprints through the desert or canoe along rivers – then lift off in a hot-air balloon!

EUROPE

Brave the wild seas, or ride the lightning bolts. Race across storm-tossed Europe to your magnificent flying machine!

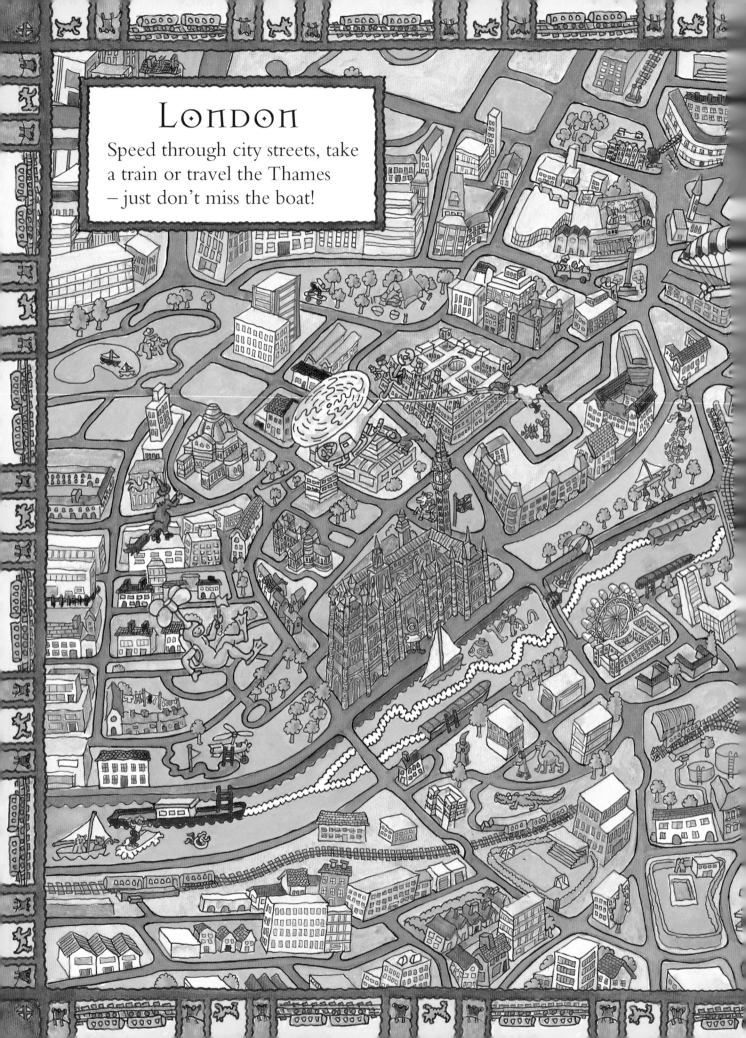

London

Speed through city streets, take a train or travel the Thames – just don't miss the boat!

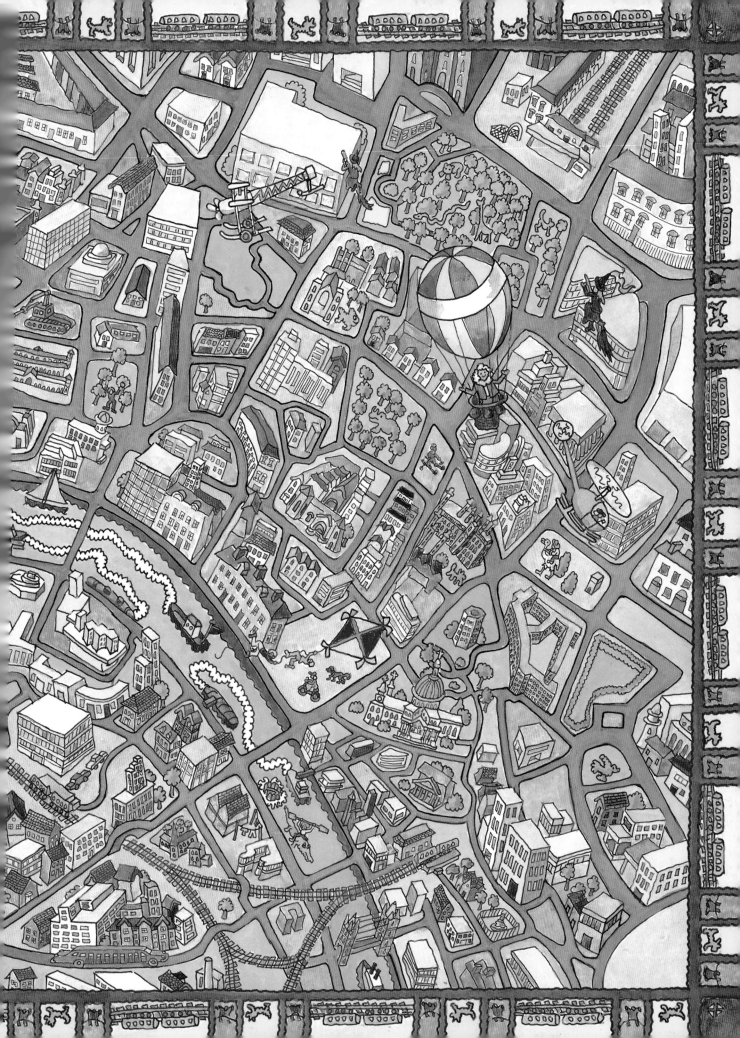

SCANDINAVIA

Go by land, sea or cable car – you have a sleigh ride waiting at the other end.

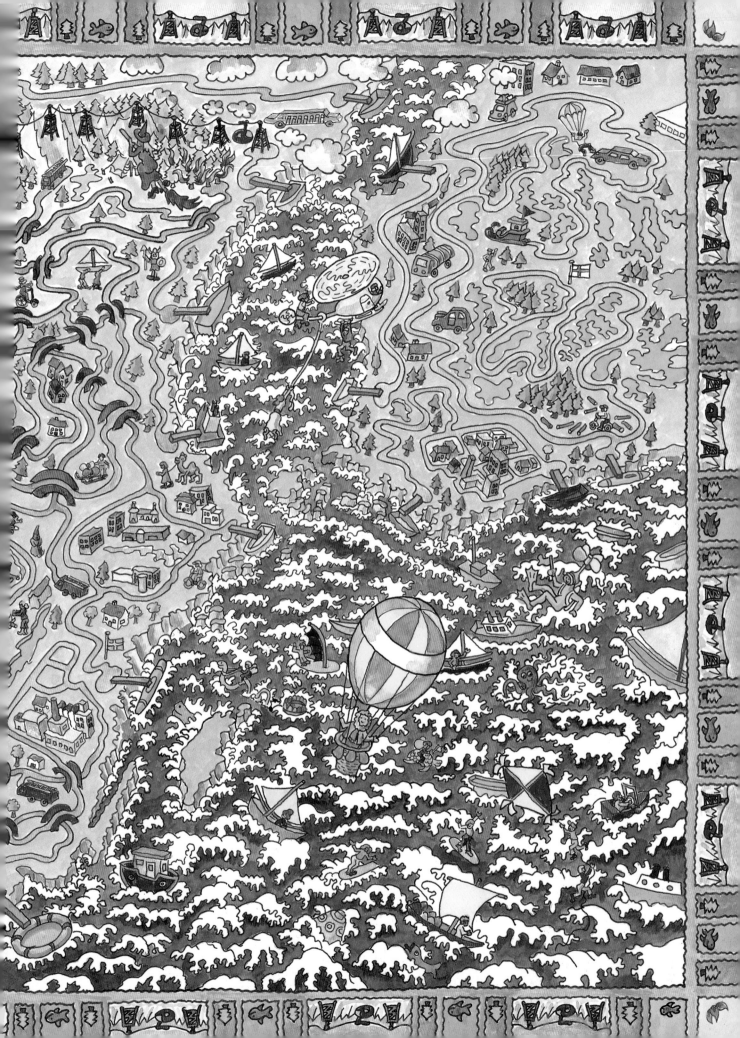

Moscow

Wrap up well and keep those sleigh bells jingling all the way to the aeroplane.

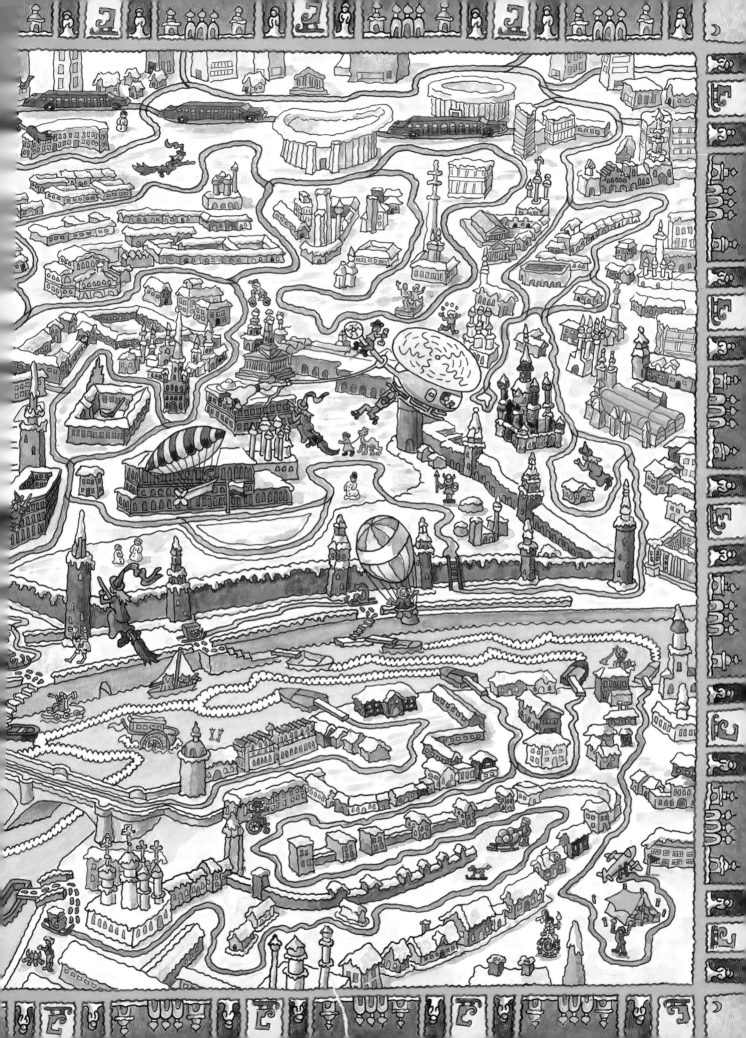

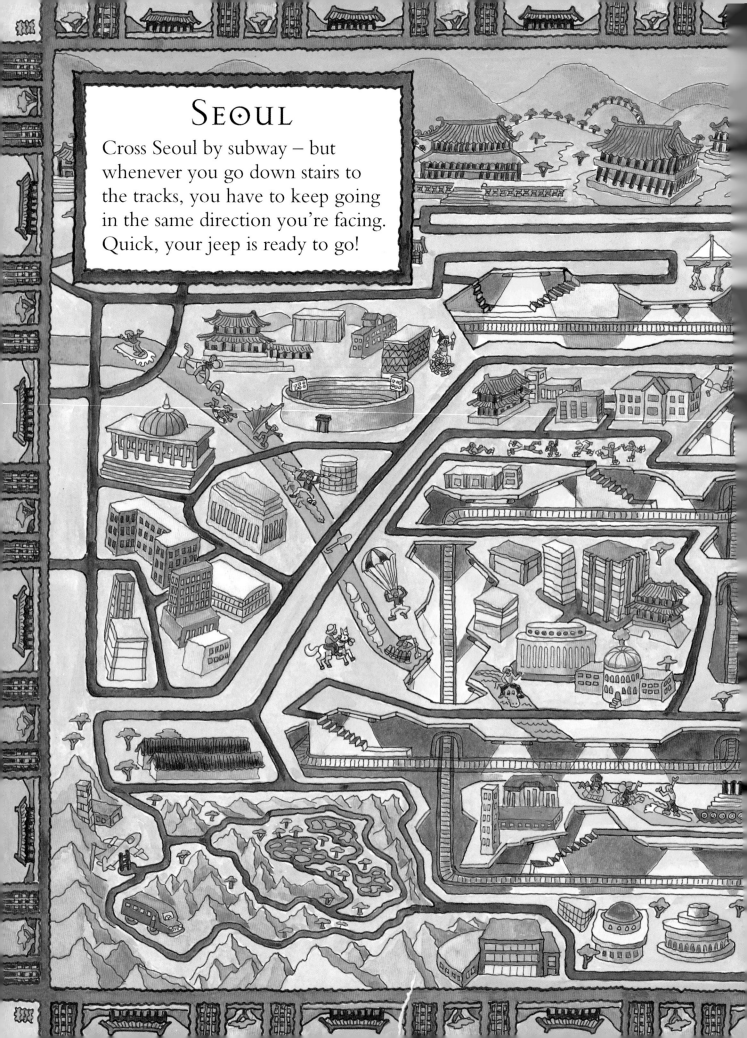

SEOUL

Cross Seoul by subway – but whenever you go down stairs to the tracks, you have to keep going in the same direction you're facing. Quick, your jeep is ready to go!

İNDİA

Beware of the tigers lurking in the grass as you follow their footsteps to the big red bus.

SYDNEY

Buzz across the busy harbour
to the final flag on the steps
of the famous opera house.
And the race is won!

Puzzles

Now you have completed the mazes, let's see if you can go the extra mile and solve these puzzles.

The Arctic

Some of the spectators have been building snow animals. How many can you find? (Don't count the polar bears!)

New York

Follow the tangled strings to find out who is holding the fish kite.

The Amazon

Who has stolen the pirate's paddle?

The Atlantic

The diver has lost one of his flippers. Can you find it?

North Africa

How many sandy snakes can you find in the desert?

Europe

Who set up the ambush that blocked the road? (Hint: Only one character could reach the ambush.)

London

How many topiary animals can you find carved in the bushes?

Scandinavia

The forest is on fire. Can you find a fire engine that can reach the fire and put it out?

Moscow

One of the witches has lost her broomstick. Find her broomstick and her black cat.

Seoul

Help the hippo rider reach the cameleer.

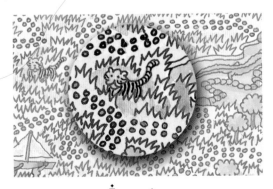

India

How many tigers can you find hidden in the grass?

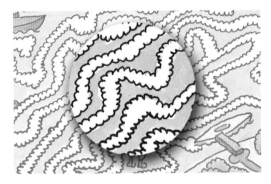

Sydney

Can you find a frothy snake hidden in the waves?

Solutions!

These are the most direct routes through the mazes.

New York

The Atlantic

The Arctic

The Amazon

Effective Communication

A guide for the people professions

2nd edition

NEIL THOMPSON

palgrave
macmillan

First published as *Communication and Language: A Handbook of Theory and
Practice* 2003
Reprinted five times
Second edition 2011
PALGRAVE MACMILLAN

Palgrave Macmillan in the UK is an imprint of Macmillan Publishers Limited,
registered in England, company number 785998, of Houndmills, Basingstoke,
Hampshire RG21 6XS.

Palgrave Macmillan in the US is a division of St Martin's Press LLC,
175 Fifth Avenue, New York, NY 10010.

Palgrave Macmillan is the global academic imprint of the above companies
and has companies and representatives throughout the world.

Palgrave® and Macmillan® are registered trademarks in the United States,
the United Kingdom, Europe and other countries

ISBN 978-0-230-24350-7

This book is printed on paper suitable for recycling and made from fully
managed and sustained forest sources. Logging, pulping and manufacturing
processes are expected to conform to the environmental regulations of the
country of origin.

A catalogue record for this book is available from the British Library.

A catalog record for this book is available from the Library of Congress.

10   9   8   7   6   5   4   3
20   19   18   17   16   15   14   13   12   11

Printed in China